A Dog Path

LEVEL 3

/th/

DECODABLES BY jump!

Teaching Tips

Yellow Level 3

This book focuses on the phoneme **/th/**.

Before Reading

- Discuss the title. Ask readers what they think the book will be about.
- Sound out the words on page 3 together.

Read the Book

- Ask readers to use a finger to follow along with each word as it is read.
- Encourage readers to break down unfamiliar words into units of sound. Then, ask them to string the sounds together to create the words.
- Urge readers to point out when the focused phonics phoneme appears in the text.

After Reading

- Encourage children to reread the book independently or with a friend.
- Ask simple questions about the text to check for understanding. Have them find the pages that have the answers to your questions.

This edition is published by arrangement with Booklife Publishing.

5357 Penn Avenue South
Minneapolis, MN 55419
www.jumplibrary.com

Decodables by Jump! are published by Jump! Library.

Library of Congress Cataloging-in-Publication Data is available at www.loc.gov or upon request from the publisher.

ISBN: 979-8-88996-801-6 (hardcover)
ISBN: 979-8-88996-802-3 (paperback)
ISBN: 979-8-88996-803-0 (ebook)

Photo Credits

Images are courtesy of Shutterstock.com. With thanks to Getty Images, Thinkstock Photo and iStockphoto. Cover – Jagodka. 4–5 –Nick Beer, Monkey Business Images. 6–7 – Hollysdogs, sanjagrujic. 8–9 – Helena56, SarahBavaria. 10–11 – Alex Zotov, Jaromir Chalabala. 14–15 – Shutterstock.

Can you find these words in the book?

bath

path

them

they

throw

with

Can they go on this path with a dog?
They can.

They go on the path with the dog.

They let the dog run and pass them.

The dog has to go to the bathroom.

They pick it up and throw it away.

This path is wet. Will the dog run on it?

He will. The wet path is fun to run on.

Get the dog in the bath!

Can you say this sound and draw it with your finger?

Trace the letters /th/ to complete each word. Say the words out loud.

bath

path

with

What other words can you spell with /th/?

pa___

ma___

Ear___

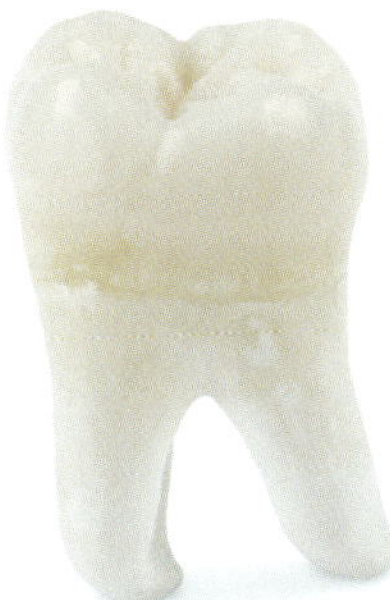

too___ ___umb

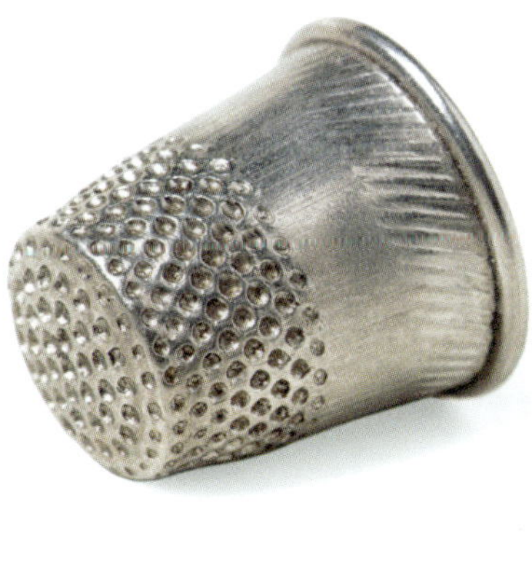

___imble

Practice reading the book again:

Can they go on this path with a dog?

They can.

They go on the path with the dog.

They let the dog run and pass them.

The dog has to go to the bathroom.

They pick it up and throw it away.

This path is wet. Will the dog run on it?

He will. The wet path is fun to run on.

Get the dog in the bath!